MY STORY

SHARON FOCKLER BARNES

DECEMBER 2020

DEDICATION

I would like to dedicate this book to my husband Michael who has always stayed beside me in sickness and health. He has always encouraged me to be who I am.

Thank you Keith, Kurt, Kris, Alan, Kevin and Joanne for making me proud to be your Mom.

Love you guys

Chapter 1

On December 29, 1941, a little girl was born to Georgia T. Fockler (Eason was her maiden name) and Floyd E. Fockler. They named her Sharon Louise Fockler. She was born just after Pearl Harbor. Mom and Dad were living with Mom's brother and Dad's sister in the house that Mom spent her teen years in. Mom's brother married Dad's sister just before Mom and Dad got married. They had some land, but no house to live in. Three years later they found out another baby was on the way, and it was getting a little crowded at Uncle Bud's and Aunt Olive's, as they had a son, Bobby, and a new baby on the way also.

Dad was always quite ingenious. He found a house that had burned and he offered to take it down if he could have the wood to build our house. He built the foundation with cement blocks, and the septic system. They were able to finish it enough so when my sister, Phyllis, was born on January 17, 1945, we moved in. The house had two bedrooms, but no bath at the time. Mom and Dad worked hard to make it a wonderful home for us. My sister still lives in the house I grew up in.

We lived in the country just across the field from my grandma and grandpa Fockler. Dad had six other siblings, one brother and five sisters. They all lived within ten miles from us, and most went to the little church on the corner nearby. It was used as a school through the week, and a church on Sunday.

My mom lost her mom when she was a teen, and her dad passed away right after I was born. She had two sisters and two brothers, the youngest one had Down syndrome and passed away right after Grandma Eason. They said it was caused by a broken heart, because he depended on Grandma for everything.

My Uncle Bud and Aunt Olive were really

close to us. I think it was because they were my mom's brother and my dad's sister. As I was growing up their six boys were like brothers to me and Phyllis.

When I was still young, my Uncle Bud got a TV set. So on most Fridays we would go over and watch "Father Know's Best", and I think the other show was "Leave it to Beaver". Aunt Olive always had a snack ready for us, and it was a special time. Dad always wanted a TV, so when I was about 13 we got one.

My aunts and uncles did a lot of things together. Ice skating, tobogganing, playing games, roller skating, playing baseball, and archery are just some of the things that I remember them doing. There was a lot of musical talent, so we would sit around and sing, and they would play the accordion, banjo, xylophone and piano. It was a great way to grow up.

Whenever the doors to the church were open, Mom and Dad would be there to do what ever needed to be done. Most of my social life was through the church. A lot of our family went to the same church, and we had a great children's ministry. Every summer we had Vacation Bible School. It was so much fun. There were plays that we did at Christmas, hay rides, and ice skating parties. Those are just a few of the things we did. When I got older, I went to Youth for Christ. It involved most of the churches around the area, so we got to get to know others our age. Once a month we would all get together, and they would have a speaker or something special. We had contests against other churches about different parts of the Bible, and how much we knew. It was kind of like Jeopardy and we had to do a lot of memorizing. I have a lot of good memories.

In the summer we would go to our grandparents once a month, and have lunch with homemade ice cream that my uncles would churn on the back porch. A game of croquet would finish up the day before we went back to church. In the winter it was board games and singing around the piano. Which was also a player piano, which us kids would take turns pumping to play O' Susana, or Tennessee Waltz. Those were the two I remember at this time. I am sure there were more .

One evening Phyllis and I were waiting for our parents to come out of the house, and I spied a pair of clippers. Grandpa had an old dog named Teddy, and I thought it would be funny to clip his tail off. In doing so, I made him mad and he bit my sister in the back of the leg. She had to get stitches in it. They asked me what happened, and I lied and said I didn't know. By doing so, I almost got Teddy killed. They figured it out, and I got a good spanking. I had a lot of those over the years. I asked Phyllis why she didn't get as many spankings, and her answer was that she saw all the trouble I got into and decided it would be better to be good.

Some of my early memories, were when I was about three. Daddy bought me my first ice skates. They had two blades, and made me feel all grown up. Daddy would go out and clean off a place on the pond that was behind our house. It was really a swamp, but I thought it was a special place, almost magical. As I look back on my life, I was really blessed to have parents who cared and were part of my life.

We lived right across the field from Grandma and Grandpa, so we spent a lot of time with them. Mom thought that any TV show with guns was off limits, but we would go visit Grandpa and he would fall asleep, then we would watch the Westerns. Grandma and

Grandpa were very caring people, and they took in missionaries, or anyone that needed a place to stay. When we would go there, it seemed Grandma always had cookies and milk ready for us. Grandpa was quite the character. He would wiggle his ears. One time, we had to go to a wedding. As kids, we were bored, but then we looked over at Grandpa, and he was wiggling his ears. I laughed so hard I couldn't keep it in, and boy did I get "the look".

I was accident prone, if there was something that could get me into trouble, I was there. Just a few things that happened through the years. Right before I was to lose my front teeth, I fell down our stairs and landed on a board that had a nail on it, and broke both of my front teeth. When I was four, mom sent me over to grandma's (just across the field) and I didn't come back right away and she found me down at the school. She brought a switch. It was a branch off of our weeping willow tree. We lived about two city blocks away, and it was a long way home. That did not stop me from doing stupid things. I tried jumping over an open well, chasing my cousins in a game of hide and seek, and fell down the middle of it. My dad came down to get me. He ripped open his arm and had to have stitches. That didn't stop me. I had to try it again over our well. I was sure I could do it this time because I was practicing jumping. Daddy left the top open to dry it out, and I looked around and saw no one in sight. So I jumped, and of course went right down it. Only this time there was no one around, and all the calling in the world didn't bring help. So one hour later (It seemed like a lifetime) Mom came to find me, and there I was. Only this time I got a good whipping.

If I was told I couldn't do something, I had to try it. One time, when my sister was sick, I took a board to put up to the window. My plan was to get up there and make funny faces. Only I didn't judge well, and the board went right through the window. Another misjudgment was when my cousin and I were on the swing. She dared me to jump off the swing, so I did, only to land on my sister who was playing in the sand. We would go to my Uncle Bud's farm and were told not to bother the cattle, but when we round them up to bring them into the barn, we would jump on them and ride them in. If we got caught, we really got it, but it was so much fun, we would try it anyway. We also would go up in the hay mound and walk across the beams from hay mound to hay mound. My cousin fell and broke his arm, and we got caught.

If there was a tree I had to climb it. There was a girl in my school that I couldn't stand. She was one of those who could do no wrong, and my mom thought I should be like her. She came over with her mom to visit and I dared her to climb this tree. It was an easy one to climb, but she got up there and couldn't get down, so I left her there. My mom was not amused.

Shortly before I turned five, they found a tumor in my leg. It was twisting my foot around, so it was hard to walk. They felt that they wanted to wait until I was older to operate on it because my bones were still soft. Some good came from it. The Red Cross took all those who were crippled to see Barnum and Bailey's Circus, and also to the Icecapades. They took us right up front so we had good seats. The doctors finally operated, and I had to stay in bed for a while. Mom had a hard time keeping me there.

Right after that, Mom had to go to the hospital, and they shipped me and my sister off to my aunts and uncles. It was my mom's sister, and they lived in the city. I hated it. My sister was little and cute, and I was bored. Uncle Kenny was a drunk. He would take my cheeks and hold them, and give me a beer-smelling kiss right on the lips. They were not too happy with me either. So they decided to send me back to my Grandma Fockler's. I was so excited so that morning as I took my suit case out and set it behind Uncle Kenny's car. Of course, he backed over it and was so mad he dragged it for 2 blocks before he stopped.

I went to a one-room-school with grades kindergarten through 12th. At recesses the boys thought it was fun to chase us with these milk snakes. They would throw them and they would wrap around us. I hate snakes to this day. It was great going to a small school, as I found out later when I was to go into 7th grade. They closed the school and sent us to Howell School, which had separate class rooms, and you had to go to different ones for different subjects . You had only a certain amount of time to get there, and our school had 3 stories, so you had to go up and down stairs. Of course the next class was clear on main floor, and then my next was on the 2nd. I had a hard time getting it straight. I always struggled with school, so when I had to go to town it just was bad. I hated it and didn't try very hard. I graduated with a C average when my sister had a B+. It seemed to come easy for her, and I struggled my whole life.

I was blessed with a great memory skill, so I memorized everything. I even won a spelling contest in the 5th grade by memorizing the whole spelling list, and then I got to go to state. I didn't make that. When going against another small school, I won a dictionary. That was a very special day for me.

Many years later, when I was working at Nabisco, they gave me a test, because packing cookies was not my best thing. They found out that I had dyslexia. So I was not dumb, I just turned everything around. When I read, I would look at the word, and if it had a "G" at the front and a "L" at the back, it was girl. I still can't spell, but I do well at numbers.

Growing up on a farm—even though there was only 15 acres—we were right next to our grandparents land and our other relatives. There were always vegetables to be picked, along with all kinds of berries. We always had chores to do. On our little farm we had chickens, a bull, a cow, rabbits, and a sheep named Freckles. We had taken in many orphan sheep from Uncle Bud, but they ether died or went back to their mom. Freckles was special. He was our pet.

One Sunday evening I was ready for church, wearing a dress that I made in 4H. I was really proud of that dress, so when Daddy sent me down to put Freckles away for the night I was not happy. I said a lot under my breath. Well, Freckles decided he did not want to go. He turned and ran, and I got my hand hung up in the rope. He dragged me up the hill, ruining my dress. Looking back on it I am sure my being mad at Daddy had a lot to do with it.

Daddy called Freckles the inspector because when we were adding on to the front of the house, he would always go up and look it over when the carpenters went home. We always tied Freckles out so he could eat grass during the day, and put him in the barn at night. Then one day he got loose and went out in the road and got hit. It broke his back bone, but we did not give up on him. Daddy built him a sling so he could walk around on his front legs, hanging from the cloths line. He finally died and it was a sad day.

One day Mom went out to feed the ducks and chickens. One of our pet ducks had binder twine sticking out of his mouth, so mom started pulling it out. By the time she got done there was a whole roll of it. We thought the duck would die, but she lived. It was amazing.

I was told when I was eight that I would get a bike. It was hard to wait as everyone of my cousins got one at a much younger age. My cousin Judy had one and she would let me ride it if I did something for her. One day our mothers were together at one of the nicer houses. They met together to do things for others, like shut-ins. They called themselves The Willing Workers. Judy decided not to let me ride her bike, so I stood in front of her as she was coming down the sidewalk and she ran into me, cutting my lip. Of course I ran into the house dripping blood all over their new white rug. After ten stitch's and many "I am sorry" repeated, my parents had to pay for the rug to be cleaned. We got an allowance every week, but mine was held back for quite a while.

Judy was older than me and I thought she was cool. So when she suggested something, I went along with it. She smoked at an early age and no one knew, except me. She tried to talk me into it, but I couldn't stand it. She called me all sorts of names, but I just couldn't do it. Then there was Bobby, my best friend at the time. He was my cousin and we grew up together. One day he built a go-kart. I was so mad that he wouldn't let me drive because I was a girl. That did it. After that we were not that close any more.

As far back as I can remember, our family always went on some kind of vacation. One year we didn't have enough money to go. Our Dad found out about a well-off man who wanted to fly his plane up to Northern Michigan, but also wanted to have his antique car up there too. So he paid Dad to drive it up there and flew the whole family back. So off we went in this old car that was fixed up like new. We were not allowed to eat anything in the car. Daddy carried us out to the car in our PJ's and we took off early in the morning. The cottage they had was up on Lake Michigan, and he paid for us to stay in a motel. It was the first one that we ever stayed in. It was quite exciting.

Our Grandmother Fockler had a brother who had a cottage on Black Lake, so one night we stayed there. That night a neighbor came over and was telling our folks about a bear that got hit by a car and was roaming the woods. The ranger was out looking for it. We were suppose to be asleep, but of course we weren't, and the cottage didn't have walls clear to the ceiling, so we heard everything. Phyllis and I were worried about that bear all night.

After a few nights up near Mackinaw city, they flew us back home. I got sick on the plane cause I had a chocolate bar in my pocket and I ate it in the plane. At least that is what I think made me sick. I have flown many times and never got sick in little planes, or big ones.

Right after our trip, our grandparents bought their own cottage on the lake and we got to go up there for two weeks every summer. Sometimes we had the cottage to ourselves, and sometimes we would have our extended family there. There were times we had as many as twenty or more people there. They slept on the porch, the floor, the beach, and in hammocks.

The cottage had three bedrooms, and of course the grownup's got first choice. Down stairs, in front of the stone fire place, there was a hide-a-bed, a chair that made into a bed. and a large glassed in porch. I loved it when everyone came. We had a large boat to go fishing and water boarding. Also a row boat that the kids could use, but we were supposed to stay close by. Of course, we had to see how far we could go without getting into trouble. So we went to the park which was ¼ of a way around the lake. And of course, we had to stop and play on the large slide and swings. We lost track of time, and the next thing we heard was my father asking what we thought were doing. The boat was off limits the rest of our stay there. When my cousins came I think we did more things to get us into trouble because there was more of us to think things up.

There were a lot of funny things that happened up there. One that comes to mind is when I was getting out of the boat and Phyllis pushed it away. There I was one foot on the dock, and another on the boat. In the water I landed, coming up madder than a wet hen. Phyllis still laughs about that. There was the time my cousin and I slept on the hide-a-bed, and my uncle thought it would be funny to fold the bed up with us in it. At the end of the bed it folded over so our feet were stuck so we couldn't get out. They let us hang there while we begged them to let us down. My one uncle liked to sleep in the hammock outside. It was one of those that had a zipper on it and we made it so he couldn't get it undone. then we hid and watched him try to get out of it. Revenge! Another time my Uncle brought up a pair of water skis. I was good at water boarding so I thought it would be a piece of cake. Well, I tried and tried to get up on them. I ended up getting rope burn between my legs. I found out you don't put the rope that close to your legs. I tried to hide it because I wanted to ski now, and I knew how, and our vacation was coming to an end. Then I got an infection in my legs so bad that I had to go see the doctor. Every year I went water skiing every chance I could. It became my favorite water sport.

When we got old enough, we were allowed to go to the little store on the corner. It was called Hank's and Vi's gift shop. They had ice cream, pop, and a lot of neat things to look at.

We would save up our allowances so we would have money to spend. Phyllis always saved more than I did. Mom always said if I had a penny in my pocket, I had to spend it. I guess that is why Phyllis is better at saving than I am.

Most days we were there, it was sunny and warm, but when it rained or was cool we would pack up and go to Mackinaw, and sometimes went to the Island. At that time there was no bridge over to the UP (Upper Peninsula) so you had to take a ferry across. We thought that was really cool. We also visited Cheboygan. Daddy liked to go down and look at all the big boats that came in off the great lakes. It was like watching the rich and how they lived. Phyllis and I have a lot of good memory's at the cottage. Later, I was able to take my children there, and Keith and Kurt talk about it. The others were young so I don't think they remember too much about it.

Another vacation we took was with my Uncle Merle and Aunt Helen. We went to the UP and spent two weeks sightseeing and camping. We had to take the ferry across. That was fun because there were two cars packed with camping equipment. Whenever we did anything with our Uncle Merle and Aunt Helen, we had a good time. We went to Sue Saint Marie Michigan and saw the boats come in and be lifted up in the canal so they could move from Lake Erie to Lake Superior. Then we went camping on Lake Superior. We had a big tent that the adults slept in with a divider in it so each couple had their own space. Aunt Helen had a little boy named Thomas, he got to sleep in the tent with them. My sister and I, along with our second cousin, slept in the back of a station wagon. Our second cousin Ruth Anne was in the middle. Phyllis slept on one side, and I slept on the other. Our cousin got sick and tried to get out on my side, leaving me covered with vomit. Then she went to Phyllis's side, doing the same. We ended up having to strip and wash in the lake. Boy was that cold. Then we had to sleep in with the adults. That was a long night. We didn't get much sleep because the guys snored.

Another memory. Lake Superior was warm that year, and that was unheard of. Aunt Helen shaved her legs in the lake, and being young, I thought it was gross. She also got upset because someone used her spatula. Not sure why that was such a big deal, but we heard about it all day.

Every summer, besides going to Black Lake, we went to Bible Camp. It was great. I got to go when I was eight. Most kids couldn't go till they were ten, but because my aunt worked at the camp, I was able to go at a younger age. I was so excited about going. Being the youngest there, I got picked on a lot. I wanted a top bunk, but because I was small, I had to take a bottom bunk. The second year, I was braver, and I was tired of being bossed around. So when this girl that slept up on the upper bunk was trying to get me in to trouble, I lifted myself up so my feet hit the bottom of her bunk, and shot her right out of the bed on to the floor. She broke her wrist, and I felt bad because I just wanted her to stop teasing me. I thought they were going to send me home, but all I had to do was clean the bathroom. It was worth it.

I went to camp till I was sixteen. At the age of eighteen, I became a counselor and found out it was not all that easy to keep twelve girls under control. It is surprising how we see things different as we grow up.

Camp was special for me, that is were I accepted Christ as my Savior. I grew up in Church, but it wasn't until then that I realized I need to ask Him to forgive me of my sins, and that it was a personal relationship. He became to mean much more to me. Praise the Lord for His unfailing love. He forgives and forgives, which is good because, as you read this, you can see I was not perfect. As days go by, I get older and realize how short life is here on earth. That I am blessed to know when I leave this earth, I will be with Him.

At eleven I had rheumatic fever, and was in bed most of the summer. The one thing I remember about the whole deal was that I couldn't stand to have even sheets touching me. The disease left me with a heart murmur. It never really interfered with anything, but every time I went to the doctors they always made a big deal about it. I sometimes wonder if that had to do with my heart problems later on.

Phyllis and I always wanted a horse, but daddy felt they were not worth feeding just for a few hours of fun. Then some new people came and moved in across the road from us. Their daughter Mary Beth had a horse that she never rode. So I went over and asked if we cleaned out the stall, could we ride the horse. They thought that was a good deal. So the next day Phyllis and I, with pitch fork and shovel in hand, went to clean out the stall. It was so full of horse manure that the horse couldn't even stand up in there. So we knew why they thought cleaning it out was a good deal. After a week of cleaning out the stall, we got to ride the horse. We had to get up on the hay wagon that was out in the field to get on the horse. We rode it bareback at least three times a week, or whenever we could get out of the house. Once I had the mumps and I was stuck in the house, so I went outside when mom was not looking and went and and rode the horse. You would think that was great, but the horse went under a branch, and I ended up in a mud puddle. So Mom found out anyway. Then Mary Beth moved, and our riding days were over. My aunt and four cousins moved in to that house, and we started a whole new adventure.

My uncle owned a jeep that he bought from the army, and he let us drive it. He thought it would help when we got our licenses. It was a lot of fun driving, and we didn't have to worry about the Police because we stayed on our land. One afternoon, my cousin dared me to drive through the pond. We made it half way and it sunk. Then we went to Uncle Glen and shared what happened. He said you got it stuck so get it unstuck. We got it out ourselves and we never did it again. We had a lot of land to run it on, and we had to stay off the roads because our parents wouldn't let us. One hot afternoon we took it to this little lake that all the kids went to. To get there, we had to go about a half mile on the road. We never got caught, but we thought Phyllis would tell on us because she did that quite often. We called her "tat a tail".

We had swamps on our land, and we were told to stay out of them. Well, it was hot, and we were with a babysitter who didn't care what we did. So I went wading in the water and stepped on a crab apple thorn. That night my foot was bright red and swollen. Phyllis wanted to tell, but I wouldn't let her. In the middle of the night I got real hot, so she went and told. I ended up having to go to the doctor because I had infection in it, and they put me on Penicillin. I was allergic to it and I ended up in the hospital. While I was there. my pet rabbit died, and daddy felt bad so he replaced him and didn't tell me. He didn't tell until I realized the new black rabbit had a small white spot on his back. Daddy came clean, and told me what happened.

I don't remember Daddy spanking me very much. Mom did all the discipline, but one day Dad asked me to do something, and I talked back to him. He came up out of that chair and marched me right in to the bedroom. He made sure I knew that was not allowed. I remember that because after he spanked me, he had tears in his eyes, and I never wanted Daddy to be upset with me again. He had a very tender heart.

When Mom got upset, Daddy would hold her and tell her he loved her until she would break down and weep. He would sometimes dance through the house, and we would laugh with him. He had a big heart, and was always helping someone out. He was a leader for 4H electronics, and he taught me how to wire a lamp and many things about electricity. One day when I five or so, I thought it would be fun to put a hairpin in an electrical plug, and I blew the breaker. My hand was black. Of course I lied, but because of my black hand I didn't get away with it. I was really good at telling lies, but Mom usually figured it out. So when I was old enough, Dad showed me a lot about electricity. His 4H class was all boys, so he taught me on the side.

Daddy loved to laugh, and we were always trying to come up with some kind of prank to pull on each other. One day, Daddy was working on a bus for our church and he had a step ladder sitting at the back of the bus. Phyllis thought it would be funny if she moved it. Well daddy didn't look and he step right off the back of the bus and landed on the ground. Phyllis felt so bad.

Daddy worked hard he was a draftsman at Howell motors, then he would come home and help Grandpa Fockler milk the cows. Daddy didn't get mad or upset over much. I asked him about it, and he told me that when he was younger he got so mad at a cow that he almost killed it with a pitch fork. He decided that every time he felt that anger, he would stop and pray. Daddy played the violin and his favorite Hymn was "The old rugged cross". I do re-member him singing "His eye is on the Sparrow" and " What a Friend we have in Jesus". Daddy touched many lives. He had a way with people. When we had his memorial service when he went to be with the Lord, there were a lot of friends there, and many testimonies about how he touched their lives and how knowing him had blessed them.

Mom was more serious. She made sure we knew how to keep house and to take care of ourselves. She also enjoyed life and she always said Daddy taught her that. She was always willing to help where she was needed. She loved working with children. She was brought up in a home that did not show love, so she worked extra hard to make sure we knew we were loved. She felt that cleanliness was next to God-liness. We were taught to keep our rooms clean and to do chores. Phyllis was better at it than I was. We shared a room, and one day Phyllis divided the room in half so I had my messy side, and she had her clean side.

I don't think I appreciated Mom. She would give her shirt off her back for you. Even though I felt she was trying to control me, she did it because she didn't want me to go through things that were hard. As it was, I ignored some of the things she tried to protect me from, and I went though them. I never heard her say I told you so.

Both Phyllis and I went to 4H. I did cooking and sewing. We had to take something to the Fair for both things, so I decided to take a cherry pie. It called for almond, and we didn't have any, so I put alum in it (that is used for pickles). Mom asked what I used because she said we didn't have any almond. So she caught it before I took it to the fair. It would have been funny if the judges would had taken a bite of that. They would have puckered up for a long time. I would have loved to seen that. Another failure was when I made my first rolls. They were so hard that the chickens wouldn't eat them.

One of the interesting things about where we lived was that there was gas in our water. It never bothered us, but when you grow up with it, you get used to it. If you lit a match under the faucet, it would burn, and at night it would build up pressure in the pipes. If you were the first one to go into the bathroom, it would shoot out of the faucet, hit the sink, and then go up in the air. No one would believe it until they saw it. Daddy called it low grade kerosene. He always thought if he could bottle it he would be rich. The school house had it too, and the kids would try and be the first to use it, just for the fun of it. Well one day our pastor (our school house was the church on the weekends), he thought he would test it out. He flushed the toilet, lit a match, and he singed his eyebrows. He was quite embarrassed to admit what he had done. All of us who lived there thought it was funny.

Christmas was a special time at our house. Mom would always make sure we had a gift under the tree. She did three gifts, one we could wear, one we had on our list, and one that was practical. I tried to do that with our children. I know they didn't have much money. Mom would go pick apples so we could have a nice Christmas. One year she picked extra so she could buy us winter coats. They were special wool coats, very nice, and we had them for a few years before we grew out of them. Some of my favorite gifts were a baby doll, a wedding doll, and a cash register (that I took apart just to see how it worked).

The most memorable Christmas was when

Phyllis and I got the Chicken Pox's a couple of days before Christmas. We were both miserable on Christmas day, and to top it all off we were not able to join the rest of our cousins and our grandparents on Christmas Eve. Christmas morning was not that exciting cause we were so sick. Under the tree were two desks, just what we wanted. I had mine for years, then I gave it to Jessica and she had it till she grew out of it. Not sure what happened with it after that. Phyllis still has hers.

On Christmas break our Uncles went to-bogganing down our favorite toboggan hill. It was at night and they couldn't see anything and they ran into a barb wire fence and they got cut up badly. Our mom and aunts were quite upset with them.

When I turned thirteen, I had a hard time with the change of going from a one room school with about twenty-five students to a High School with over two-hundred. Also, I couldn't find my place to fit in. I really didn't have any friends there, and even when I graduated six years later, I only had a couple. Friends were always important to me. My closest friend went to another school in Fowlerville just down the road from us. When the state divided up the county, their house was on the other side, and they went to a different school. It was smaller, and I think I wouldn't have minded it as much.

One of the things with the new school, no more overalls. We had to wear skirts or dresses. Well, I had tons of hair on my legs, and Mom didn't want me to shave them. She said once you start, you have to keep it up. I didn't understand that statement as I was getting teased about how much hair I had. I would have done anything. Then one day I was over to my grandmas and my Aunt Vivian was there (she was only 10 years older than I was). She helped me by getting me some hair remover. It didn't work very well, and so I had spots that the hair didn't come off. It looked worse than when I just had the hair. Mom was not happy, but she let me shave, and they looked great. She was right, you do have to keep it up, but it was worth it.

Chapter 2

Most of those in High School had an idea what they wanted to do after graduation. But for me, all I wanted was to get married, have children, and live happily ever after. First, I didn't have a boyfriend or even had anyone act like they wanted to take me out. Daddy said I couldn't date till I was 16, but it would have been nice to have someone act like they liked me. I had a crush on a boy named Junior in our church. I was involved in Youth for Christ and he was in it too. My Uncle Merle and Aunt Helen were our youth group leaders. We did a lot of fun things with other churches.

One night we went as a group to eat pizza.
Now, I grew up with my cousins, and we always
tried to out-eat each other. Well, I wanted to
show off for Junior, so I ate until I was almost
sick, then he turned to me and said he wouldn't
want to take me on a date. It would cost too
much. I was so embarrassed that I never
wanted to see him again. That took care of
that.

Then one Halloween, a new boy came on
the hay ride, and we talked all night. The next
day he called for a date. I was not to turn 16 for
another couple of months, but Daddy wouldn't
change his mind. So Dan and I talked on the
phone and got to know him. He was not bad to
look at, and he also was on the football team. I
thought I was falling in love with him. We
dated for 4 years, then he left and for Prairie
Bible Institute in Canada, and I went to Grand
Rapids. So I decided to break up, so we could
look around, but after a year I didn't have one
date, so when he came and asked me to marry
him, I said yes.

We had a May wedding, and we had it at the
Nazarene campus. Two things I remember

about my wedding. One, Mom was late. So we had to wait for her to be seated before we came down the aisle. And the other thing was that Dan's brother Duane was asked to move his little Volkswagen, and he backed it in to a telephone pole.

For our honeymoon, we borrowed Uncle Merle's Volkswagen van and went to the Smokies. It was the first time I had seen the mountains and I was awed by them. We camped out in the van.

We bought a trailer to live in, and had it put on Nazarene Campground. It was 8 feet wide and 35 feet long. One day Dan and I drove down to the lake to go swimming. On our way Dan says did you know Volkswagens float? I said, no way! Well he drove that car right into the lake and it floated, but it was heading for the dock. So he told me to get out and pull the car back in to shore. First of all, it was a convertible, and he had me climb out the window. Then when I got in close to the shore, it sunk because the motor was in the back. He got upset, opened the door, and let the water into the car.

At the time it was not funny, but now I crack up every time I remember it. The other thing that was funny was that they threw rice at us when we got married. This was only a few weeks after, so the rice that got down in places we didn't know about, and swelled up and stunk. It took a few cleanings before we got it out.

We lived in the little trailer for two years and moved when Keith was one year old. We moved to a house built inside of a hill. We had more space than we knew what to do with.

There, the house was on top of the hill, and I had a garden at the bottom. One fall, Keith and I went down to get the last of the garden. Keith was three, and I was pregnant at the time. We were coming up the hill, and Keith ran around the back of the house and disappeared. I could not find him anywhere. We lived right on a main road, and I was scared he would get out in the road. Then I thought about the river that ran not that far behind our house, and that really freaked me out. So I called my dad, who worked not far away, and he came to help me find him. We were ready to call the police, when a car passed, then came back, and a man asked if we were looking for a little boy. He told us the boy was up on the next hill without a stitch of clothing on. That was a scare, so the next weekend both our parents came over and put a childproof fence up. They put up a swing set, and a sandbox. Then they came in to eat supper. We looked out the window and saw Keith go over the fence. Child proof it was not.

Kurt was born there, and we stayed until he was one, then we moved to Webberville into a two bedroom house. It was smaller, but we were closer to Dan's work in Lansing. We were there for a couple of years, then Dan decided to go back to Three Hills, Canada. So we put the house up for sale.

That's when I found out I was going to have another baby. I wanted so badly to stay because both my parents and his were close by. Then my appendix broke, and I had to have surgery. The baby and I made it through fine. Three months later Kris was born in Canada. We did not sell the house, and I was sure we wouldn't move to Canada, but we did. We took off in a truck with a truck camper on it, and a trailer with all our earthly possessions.

A few facts about our trip, we spent the night at a camp ground and our cat got out and we never found him. The boys cried and cried. We even spent an extra night there just in case he came back. We ate in our camper most of the time, but one night I was extra tired and felt bad, so we went out to eat. The next morning I woke up with sores in my mouth, by the time we made it to Alberta Canada, they were clear down my throat. Along with being pregnant and not being able to swallow, I ended up in the hospital. In the meantime Dan found a basement apartment, and they moved in. What a mess I found when I came home. Luckily, I only had to stay one night. The apartment had one bedroom, a small sitting room, and a kitchen. It came furnished, so we had to just move in.

We got to Canada at the end of October, and Kris was born on December 17th. We went to the mountains to find a Christmas tree, and I started into labor. I just made it to the hospital in time. So now we had five of us sleeping in one room. Very cozy, we had bunk beds, our bed, and a baby bed that I brought with us.

The people who lived upstairs were from Africa, there were three girls who would jump off the couch, and the boys called them the jumping kangaroos. Just after we moved there, I sent Keith off to school and thought he was dressed warm enough, but he froze his feet just walking one block to school. So we had to get mukluks and parka's for them to keep them warm. The sun was shining that day, but it was minus thirty degrees. I had no idea it was that cold.

Sleeping in one room had its challenges. I had a baby who woke up every hour, and of course he had colic. I spent a lot of nights in the kitchen as it was the farthest from the bedroom. The other two boys were on the bunks. Keith was on the top, and one night he got up, and was walking back and forth across the top. By the time I realized what was happening he walked right off the top and landed on our bed. He split his lip open and spent the night in ER, sporting stitches. We were blessed to have a wringer washer there in the basement and a place to hang the laundry. It saved us a lot of money.

Six months later we moved into base housing. It was set up like a motel with a bath house just down the walkway. There were ten units per row, and there was two rows. Each unit had a big room with a kitchen on one wall, and a couch on the other, with a table in the middle. It had two bedrooms that were just big enough to hold a full bed, with no room to spare. So we built bunks for the boys, with the crib as the bottom bunk, and the other two were above that. So that gave us room for a dresser, which I used the bottom drawer for the few toys they had. In our room we put pegs on the wall to hang things on, and a box under the bed for things that could not be hung. It was quite cozy.

I was given a tub for the boys, because they only had showers in the bath house. Until I got the tub, I gave them their baths in the kitchen sink. One day I had to go grocery shopping, and Dan stayed home. I put the boys in the tub as they liked playing, and I wasn't going to be that long. When I came home, there were the boys still playing, only this time they were joined by salamanders (they look like small lizard's). Of course I freaked. They ended up having to take another bath. They could not understand why I got so upset. They would find them in the desert, and would bring them home. I always made them keep them outside, at least until that day, and that was the last one too.

Dan didn't care for living that close to others, so we found a farm house about two miles away to rent. It had three bedrooms, and lots of room. It was nice for when it got so cold the kids couldn't go out. They had lots of room to play. A couple of downers were we had to buy water and have it delivered to a cistern. The other was the coal furnace feeder would jam up when the coal froze. So I would have to go down and shovel it out of the bin and let it dry on the floor before I could put it in the hopper. I would make the boys sit on the stairs when I did that so I could keep an eye on them.

Keith was the only one in school and he rode the bus. We laughed because the land was so flat we could see the bus at least 20 minutes before it got to our house. Also, there was a turkey farm across from the house and they would give us free eggs. They were okay. Not great for fried eggs, but for scrambled and baking, they were great. The boys really enjoyed it there.

The next place we lived at for only three months. It was in Calgary in a basement. We had an Irish Setter dog. The day we moved down from Three Hills we decided to go out. So we locked him in the kitchen, and when we got back there, he was sitting at the door. Then we went down stairs and saw that he had chewed his way through the kitchen door.

The basement was very small so we started to look for a place the kids could play outside. We found one. It was a small house with two bedrooms and about as big as the motel rooms were. It had a nice yard, which the boys enjoyed. Kris was about three at the time, and we left him and his brothers with a neighbor so we could go out with friends. (which we never did) I was so uneasy all night, and when we got home we found out Kris had had a seizure. He ended up spending some time in the hospital. I never left them again until they were older. Another time the boys were chasing Kris, and he ran right into an unopened can of paint. It split his head open. Back to the ER and a few stitches. Poor guy. It seemed he was always getting hurt.

Kurt was the other one who was accident prone. His dad took him and his brothers sledding, and he came home with a large cut above his eye. I thought he needed stitches, but Dan thought just a band aid would do. I think he still has a scar there.

Dan got a job as an electrician to work in Banff national park at the Grand Hotel. We got to go stay there as it was closed down, and had to eat out or make sandwiches in our room. Breakfast was easy, but we did get tired of peanut butter. So the kids and I would go down to the Chinese place, and I would order a bowl of wonton soup. All three of us would eat off of it, and I would take the rest to Dan. It worked out quite well. The kids and I only stayed for two weeks, as they got bored. There was not a lot to do. It was in the off season, and a lot of the things were closed.

We bought a new sixty by twelve mobile home and parked it in a trailer park in High River. We were there for two years. It was a nice place to live. Of course we didn't stay there, so then we went to Blackie. It was a small town and we rented a spot to park the trailer. Then Dan bought a lot, and we were there just a short time before we moved again. Let's see, that is number seven since we landed in Canada, not counting when we moved twice in Blackie.

Kurt started school there and he always took naps at home. I never asked him to, but at one o'clock every day he would take a nap wherever he was. He had only been in school a couple of weeks, and I get a call from the teacher explaining that was not going to work. He was going in the afternoon, so they moved him to the morning. I was told I needed to break the habit as he was going all day the next year.

The other thing that happened there was we had a tent trailer camper and we never left it set up. But one day we did, and the wind came up, and blew it down the road, right it to another persons yard. It was never right after that.

Once we went camping in the mountains on Easter weekend, and I hid the Easter baskets in the trees. Well, Kurt never did find his. We think a bear took it, but not sure. It started snowing, so we packed up and tried to get out of there. But the car wouldn't move so. the boys and I tried to push it, and we got covered with mud. We drove all the way home wet and muddy. Before we left Canada we had moved fourteen times. The kids and I were tired of moving.

One Christmas I decided to to buy a tree because the roads were bad, and it didn't look like we would ever get out to get one. Three days later I got up and all the needles were off the tree. So my good deal was not all that it was cracked up to be. The next day I went and got another one, at least this one lasted through Christmas.

Mom and Dad came to visit us and went camping with us. The first time they rented a camper so they didn't have to pull one clear up to Canada, but the second time they brought their own. We had a great time camping with them. Kris was about two and he loved to ride his bike through the water puddles. We were getting ready to go some place and I told him to stay inside while I got dressed. As you know we always don't do what we are told. He went right out to the puddle. Daddy saw him and told him to get back in to the house, well it just broke Kris's heart that his grandpa scolded him for doing that. It was great having family visit. Dan's parents came a couple of times also.

On one of our trips through Banff National Park, we took our Siamese cat with us camping. We had our tent trailer and she was pregnant. We didn't want to leave her home. I think my parents were with us, but they had their car and trailer. Anyway, the cat had her kittens on the floor of our car, and the boys got a lesson on how babies are born. Later after we camped, we made a bed for her and her kittens. She left them for a while, then didn't seem to be able to find them. We had to help her to come home. She was a good mother.

We didn't have a phone most of the time. Because it was expensive to call back to the US, we sent cassettes back and forth. It was great hearing our family's voices and the boys loved talking to their grandparents. I wish now I would have kept them, it would be great to hear their voices.

Our next move was to McKenzie, British Columbia. We took our sixty foot trailer. It was nerve-wracking as we watched the trailer go through the mountains. We were on the road only a short time and the front side of the siding on the trailer came off. That was sad, as it never got fixed, and it didn't look that good. It was an interesting place to live and so far North that everything was expensive. A head of lettuce was $3, and milk was $5 a gallon. So every three months we would go to Prince George, and get groceries. They had to last us for three months, so at the end of three months I had to be creative.

We were only in McKenzie for a year and half, but were there for two winters. The boys loved the snow. It started snowing in September and didn't stop till May. The boys built an igloo, which was quite impressive and lasted all winter. For entertainment we would go to the dump and watch the bears. We were far enough away to see them, but not in any danger. There were no snow days, but when the temp got below -30 the kids got to stay home. But then it was too cold to play outside. So we were all in that 60' by 12' trailer. We put a wood stove in it because we couldn't keep it warm otherwise, and played a lot of games and puzzles.

Next we moved our trailer onto some land just outside of Grand Prairie. The first place we lived was in the middle of a field. Right after we moved there, Kevin decided to make a grand entrance. Right after he was born, my Daddy went to be with the Lord. We flew back to Michigan for the memorial service. It was a sad time as Mom was having a hard time with the loss of Dad. We all did, because he was the light to our home.

In Grand Prairie we were on a hill and got all the wind and cold. We were on the edge a wild life preserve so there were lots of geese and ducks. There were a lot of interesting birds. There was a pond there, and once in awhile they would come with an airboat and would go to look at things on the water. They would take the boys out on it. They thought that was cool.

We had bought some land, but had to wait until they brought in electricity. We also needed a well. So for a month we dug out a well. It was four by four and we dug it forty feet deep. We rigged up a bucket on a pulley, and the boys and I would bring it up out of the hole, and run it down the hill and dump it. When we finally we hit water, it was so exciting, but the boys and I were tired. When we moved the trailer over to the land, we still had to use an outhouse, but we could use the tub and sinks.

We wanted to build a log house on there, so we found a place that would cut the logs to the right size, and we just had to put it together. It was like putting a puzzle together. They were heavy, and the kids and I had a hard time moving them, even though Dan made a lift out of chains.

My mom came to visit right when we were trying to get it done. That was a blessing, as she watched Kevin, who was a baby. I know it was a hard time for her, as she had just lost Daddy. I asked her one time if she ever thought of getting married again, and she said she had the best, and didn't think she could replace him. I agree Daddy was one of a kind.

We got the house up by the end of August, but we still had to do the roof. We ended up in a time crunch. Dan had sold the trailer and we had to be out of it by October. I went to church, and someone asked how the house was coming. I told them. Well, the next week a group from church came out and put the roof on and shingles. What a blessing that was. Well, the time was close for them to come and get the trailer. We didn't have windows yet. So we put plastic on the windows, and moved in. Of course the temperature dropped and we couldn't keep it warm with the wood stove. We slept around the wood stove, and we stayed close by, just to keep warm. A neighbor came over and saw what was happening, and took the children to her house. Dan was working away from home, so I stayed at the house trying to keep it warm. The next week we were able to put the windows in and move everyone back home. We never did get the septic in, so we used an out house and port-a-potty at night.

Next we moved back to Michigan. Dan felt he wanted to live up North, so we bought a house in Cheboygan. It was a cute house made all out of stone. We had a stone fire place and a stone barn (at least on the bottom) and a stone shed.

We did a haunted house in the barn at Halloween, and the kids loved it. Did a maze with bails of hay, and had things hanging from the rafters. The boys loved doing it.

I once asked the boys to watch Kevin, who was only two while I ran into the house. When I came out he was gone and so was the dog. I found their foot marks in the snow. So off I went to find them. The only thing, the snow was deep and Kevin and the dog could walk on top of the snow, but I kept falling into the snow, so it made it hard to walk. Finally I saw them Kevin was sitting on a log talking to the dog. I was so happy to see them.

Kevin was young, so if we didn't watch him he could get himself in to a lot of trouble. One day I went to check on him, and Kurt's pony had him by the seat of his pants just hanging there. It was funny, Kevin was laughing so he was not hurt. The house was cute, but had some extra guests. Keith had his bedroom in the basement and he could hear critters all night long. So could Kurt who was out on the porch. Well one day we had to get up in the eaves and found out that there were thousands of bats living in our house. When we opened up the wall they flew out to the trees just across the road from us.

Dan decided he didn't want to live there anymore, so he flew out to Portland Oregon to see if he could find a job there. He told me that after I sold the house to pack up everything and move out there. I didn't want to go, so I didn't put the house up for sale. I started to run out of things to sell, and I tried to find a job, but that didn't work. So I put the house up for sale, and it sold with in a week. The Realtor said she was surprised that it went that fast as some others were up for months and hadn't sold. The boys didn't want to move again, but the schools were bad, so it was a good move. I think they liked it.

Dan's mom rode out to Oregon with me to help with the children. I was so glad to have an extra set of eyes and helping hands. We didn't get off to a very good start, I drove up to the Phillips place and somehow our dog, Buttons, got out. We had been gone for quite a while, when the boys noticed he was gone, so we turned around and headed back. There stood Grandpa with this look on his face, and he opened the door and Buttons ran right out and got into the van. We never had a problem after that. Whenever we headed to the van, Buttons would beat us there.

When we got to Oregon I didn't have a very good idea where the place was. I knew I had to go up Vernonia highway and turn off on Chapman. I was really concerned on how to find it, as Dan didn't have a phone up there, and I had no way to call. Then I noticed these paper plates on trees saying we were on the right path and we were getting close. I was praising Dan for thinking of doing a helpful thing, when I realized I had gone too many miles, so I turned around, and for some reason I picked the right road, and we made .

Chapter 3

After a few years the boys and I were on our own. I got a job with Nabisco, so we were able to make it. The boys loved the fact we didn't have to move every year or so. Also, the three older boys graduated in the same school they started High School in. Keith graduated and went into the Air Force. That was always his dream. It was a good start into life in the real world without Mom. It ended up that five of Michael's and my children went into one of the services.

One day I got a call from the Middle School saying Kurt had gotten hurt and need to go to the ER. What happened was he was swinging on a wire off the bleachers and the wire broke. He came flying down, fell flat on his face, and arm. He broke his arm and had to have gravel removed from his face. He was supposed to take it easy, but one day I couldn't find him, and he was hanging by his broken arm up a tree. He decided to built a tree house. Not sure where he gets these crazy ideas.

We had seven acres to roam around in, with government land behind us. They were given old motor cycles and they would get them running. Then they would die again and they would fix them. It kept them busy and they loved it. In the winter they would sled down the steep hill when there was snow. It was dangerous, and that is why they loved it. It is a wonder they didn't end up with broken arms or legs or other parts.

Kurt got his drivers license on Wednesday. I let him take the car on Thursday to go sign up for school. I went to bed, as I had worked all night. Kurt woke me up and told me he had rolled my car, and totaled it. He cut his arm, so his friend took him to ER. I had a friend take me to find the car, and have it towed. I was able to use their car, so I didn't lose work and and have to find a new car right away.

It was during that time that I met Sue. She worked at the 7-Eleven store that I stopped at on my way home from work to get a soda in hopes to keep me awake. She has a son and two daughters. The son, Benjamin, was the age between Kris and Kevin. So he fit right in. He would come home with them on the bus and spend time with the boys. They would keep life interesting. One night I got a call at work telling me they broke my coffee table in half. They had been messing around and Ben landed on it. So I made them pick strawberries to help replace it. I never did replace it, but at least there was a consequence for what they did.

Sue and I became best friends, and we still are. It was because of her I started square dancing. I loved it a lot, but after I married Michael we never did much. Then I had my heart problems, and couldn't do it anymore. Matter of fact, I met Michael at a square dance in St. Helens at a strawberry dance.

I feel bad sometimes as I look back on that time in our lives that I didn't do much with the children. We did go to the theater in St. Helens once in awhile. One time I was sitting on the aisle seat, looked down, and saw a rat eating something. I never wanted to go after that. We did go to the pool once in a while too.

I took a week off of work and took the boys camping. I didn't have a tent so I borrowed a couple. When we set them up, they were really small, so the boys slept in the pup tent, and Kevin and I slept in the other. Well the next day we were told we could have only one tent on a tent spot and that I would have to get another spot for the other tent. So I took both tents and but them together and made one tent. They never said anything. Sometimes when you don't have much money you have to be inventive. I think I got that from my dad. I am so glad he taught me about electric motors and how to fix things. One day my dryer stopped and I went down and got a new heating unit and put it in. Then the washer lost a belt that ran the drum, and I was able to replace that. There have been many times I was able to fix things or do things to help us without it costing us a lot.

I had borrowed a canoe and a truck from Dan so we could go fishing and paddle around the lake. We had a lot of fun and some sun burns. When I got back Dan wanted his truck back right now. I had worked all night and was tired and not a happy camper. He left that truck out there all the time so now he wanted it. He was also supposed to see the boys that weekend. So I loaded up Kevin and Kris (Kurt was of age that he didn't have to go if he didn't want too). On our way over I got hit by a car, and it threw Kris into the window. Dan was not happy, as it totaled the truck. I ended up taking Kris to the ER and have the glass picked out of his forehead. Kevin didn't get hurt because I put my arm out to catch him. There were no seat belts in the truck. It would have been good if there had been.

As I said, I met Michael at a square dance in St. Helens. He was only to be in town a short time, so we went on two dates and he left. We ended up spending a lot of time on the phone. One day he said he sent me tickets to fly down to Mississippi to go to a dance with him, and to get to know him. I flew down and we had a great time. It was then that he asked me to marry him. I wasn't sure as he was a lot younger than me. We wrote a lot of letters and he started to send me statistics on why a women being older was not a bad thing. After awhile I decided to give it a chance. I fell in love with him. He was kind, understanding, and he didn't put me down.

So April 6th, 1984 we got married in Mississippi. We did it there because he was going to Germany, and for me to go we had to be married for so many days. Our honeymoon was in Pensacola Florida. Not what you would call a very romantic one, but I got to know Alan and Joanne better. We took Michael's van and went camping. The first night it was raining, so all four of us slept in the van. The next day we did a little sight seeing. I remember we all fed the raccoon's and they came right up on the picnic table and wanted to take our food. We all laughed at them. I stayed a week then had to go home and back to work. The plan was that I was going to sell the house and then quit my job while he was in school. Then he would go on to Germany and send for us when he found us a place to live.

So in June when he brought Joanne and Alan up to stay with me while he did his schooling we did a renewing of our vows with family and friends . My pastor did it this time and we had about 30 there. To me that was when we really got married. As it was, the Air Force changed their minds and wanted him to come back, so they could plan his next assignment. Which they didn't do until a year later. This caused all kinds of problems, as I didn't want to sell the house or quit my job until we knew what was happening.

To keep his base housing he had to have one of the children live with him. So Kurt went down to Mississippi, as he was the only one graduated and had time to go. That was what gave him an insight to what the Air Force was like. Later he joined. He retired, and now has a great job with Civil Service. A year later they sent Michael to a tiny island in Alaska. We were married two years and I saw him less than a month.

It was a big adjustment for all of us. Alan and Joanne had lived in the city before they came to live with me, and we were ten miles out of Scappoose. They had to deal with three brothers (Keith had already left for the Air Force. He had planned it for a long time). Poor Joanne was the only girl so they did a lot of picking on her. If I remember right, Kris would stand up for her.

I let each child pick out whatever cereal they wanted. So Joanne picked Coco Puffs. The next morning she went to get some and someone had replaced it with dog food. We never did figure out who did it. Being that the boys had each other, I decided to get her a cat. As it ended up she had kittens. So we ended up with a lot more than what we planned. We had a Saint Bernard named Bags. He was loved and part of our family, but one day he came up missing and we never did figure out what happened to him. I think someone came up with a pick-up, and Bags loved to ride, so he just went with them.

I was so excited to have a little girl to make dresses for and to do all the girly stuff with, but as it turned out she would rather wear jeans and be one of the boys.

I was still working at Nabisco and I had five of our six children. In a way it was a good thing, because Joanne and Alan got a chance to spend time with me and bond with me. I am not sure how that would have worked if Michael and I were trying to make a marriage work. I can't say it was easy, but we have been married thirty-five years, and it will be thirty-six on April 6, 2020.

Michael has become my best friend, and someone I can share with. He takes good care of me. My love for him has grown beyond anything I could hope for. We have a good life.

When Michael finished his time in Alaska we went to a base in Michigan. It was in the UP and we were only six hours away from my mom and sister. We were stationed at KI Air Force Base for eight years. It was great being close to family. So we packed up, leaving Keith and his wife with the house and land. We packed all our belongings into a U-Haul and took off for a long trip across to Michigan. Michael drove the U-Haul, and Kris drove the van most of the time. He loved driving and it gave me a break. I had worked night shift almost right up until we left, and then packed everything up. I was tired. It soon became boring, so we stopped at Wall-Mart and I bought yarn, needles and a book on crocheting. By the time we reached Michigan I almost had an Afghan finished.

To save money we camped our way across. After the first night of everyone setting up their own tent, Joanne decided to sleep in the van and the boys opened the back of the U-Haul and slept in there. Michael and I were the only ones that set up a tent up every night. After we got to Michigan we had to camp for a few days before we could get into base housing. It took the boys three hours to unpack the U-Haul versus a whole week to pack it. Then we took off and went to see my mom, sister, and her family in lower Michigan. It was the first time Michael got to meet them. On the trip down we stopped at a picnic spot on Lake Michigan and went swimming. Kris was still with us, so he got to go and see the place and everyone. I think it was the last time he was there. Shortly after he flew back to Oregon to find a job. He lived with Keith until he could afford his own place.

We did a few camping trips each year. It was fun but I would tease Michael as he would call and say it is suppose to be nice this weekend, how about going camping. Then he would say, you and the kids pack up and I will meet you there. It seemed like he would show up after we got everything set up. Hmm?

We did a lot of shore fishing, and on creeks. The only fishing I did was in a big boat with comfortable chairs. So to make a long story short, I spent most of my time getting line out of the trees. Michael helped some, but he even got tired of doing it. I think he would rather have had me stay at camp rather than fish.

One summer we decided to go the Dells in Wisconsin so the kids could go on these water slides. After a day of play and sunshine we found a camping place and set up our tents. During the night it rained so hard that the kids tents leaked and they were soaked. We had a large air mattress and we just floated. They all came to our tent but after a short while we realized that it was not going to stop. So we all packed up, throwing all the wet camping gear in the back of the van, and headed for hot chocolate. We were a sorry sight, five soaked bodies in McDonald's, and got laughing and couldn't stop.

My first granddaughter Jessica was born and I wanted to meet her. She was going to have her first Birthday so I packed up Alan, Kevin and Joanne. Michael couldn't get time off so we took off in the van to Oregon. Alan just got his drivers license so I let him drive a lot so he could get practice. There was a lot of open road so he got lots of practice. Joanne and I camped with a tent and the boys slept in the van. We stopped at KOA camp grounds to spend the night. They had large water slide and the kids wanted to go on it. The wind came up so strong that they had to close it down. I set the tent up using the van for a wind breaker. Joanne and I didn't get much sleep that night as we thought the tent was going to take off with us in it. The next day I fell a sleep while Alan was driving (I always drove by the big city's). We were coming into Spokane and Alan woke me up asking what to do because he took the wrong exit and ended up downtown. He got so upset he stopped in the road and climbed out and told me to drive. We made it out okay, but he wouldn't drive for a while. I told him not to worry about it. It all was good.

We spent two weeks with Keith and family it was great. Getting to know my granddaughter gave me lots of joy. Keith invited everyone for a picnic so I got to see everyone. Dan came with his wife and so Kevin got to see them. Then we had to go back. I think it took longer to come back than to go.

I decided to work out at the gym and to do

some cross country skiing. I really enjoyed it. Then one day I was told I needed doctors permission to work out on the weight machine. I put it off as long as I could, then they wouldn't let me in the gym until I got a letter from the doctor. So I went and he said I was good, but I had to have a stress test. The next day I went and they didn't let me stay on the treadmill very long. They laid me down and put a white pill under my tongue. The nurse came in and said I could get dressed and left. So I left and went shopping and picked up the kids and did a bunch of errands. When I got back to the house I found out everyone was looking for me as the doctor called Michael to talk to him and me what was going on. They thought they saw something and wanted me to fly to San Antonio TX to a hospital there. I was sure nothing was wrong, but we went anyway. A funny part was we were on a medical plane and Michael didn't fly well so he took Dramamine. He was out the minute we got into our seats. The nurse came along and wanted to know why he was flying to the hospital and I told her I was the patient and he was there for support. She looked at him and said I feel sorry for you.

We were only married five years when I had a heart attack while they were giving me a heart-cath. I ended up having three open heart surgery's in a 4 month period. Then in 1991 they said there was nothing they could do, and I only had about six months to live. Well, twenty-nine years later, a pacemaker, three stints, and a lot of hospital stays, I am still here. I thank the Lord for our six children, twelve grandchildren, and five great grandchildren. Now that we live close, I am able to spend sometime with a lot of them.

I got really sick for a while, and it was hard to even get out of bed but I came up with an idea. Now I just had to talk Michael into it. I wanted a dog. I thought that would make me get out of bed and have companionship when everyone was gone. So, as usual Michael doesn't do things like I thought, so he sent me with my friend to visit her mom. On the way there she said her uncle had some puppy's. She had to bring one back for a friend, and would I help pick it out. Well it was for me, and it was an Australian puppy. It was cute, but I was thinking of a small dog. Well, she dropped me off at home and I told Michael how cute he was. She took him home, then Michael told me it was my dog. He turned out to be a great dog and we named him Chips. He loved to play catch and Frisbee. When he would fetch a ball it came back all slobbery, so Michael found a tennis racket at a yard sale. Chips would put the ball on the racket. Michael would hit it out in the field, and Chips would go running after it. He loved to play and he minded really well. One day when we were in Wyoming a farmer offered money for Chips, he said he would make a great cattle dog. We would have never taken it, as Chips was part of the family.

During our time at KI Sawyer Kurt had a remote so Sheryl and our granddaughter Kristin got to come and stay with us. Kurt was to come back and be stationed at KI. It was a wonderful time with Kristin, she was just two when she came. She had puffy little cheeks with dimples. She wasn't shy and made herself right at home. Kristin came to us just as she turned two, so I got to give her a Birthday party. I invited friends who had children her age. Even though her and mama didn't know them, she fit right in. I got two years with her and her parents. It was a special time for me. One of my fond memories is when she sang Jesus Loves Me with me at the Mothers Day luncheon. Sheryl got to come and see it. It was so precious I will never forget that day. Whenever Sheryl would give Kristin a bath Kristin would run out of the bathroom and say "look, I am all clean and fresh". Kurt and Sheryl had their second daughter at KI. She was the only grandchild that I was there for their birth. They left to move to California when she was six months.

In 1994 Michael retired from the Air Force after putting in 23 years. The base was closing and we decided it was time. Not sure how long I had here with everyone, so we decided to get a 5th Wheel and travel for a while as the kids were living all over, and I thought it would work out to spend time with all of them. God had different plans. We had to stay for the summer closeby as Michael had a lot of vacation time. He really didn't retire until the end of the summer.

So we worked at Lake Lundgren Bible camp for the summer. Michael enjoyed it so much that we joined a group called Sowers On Wheels. We spent a lot of time working at churches and Bible camps. In the summer we worked at Lake Lundgren Bible Camp in Wisconsin, and in the winter we would go south and worked where it was warmer. California was great as I got to spend time with Kurt and his family. By then he had Kristin and Kourtney.

We would make sure we got to spend time with Katie and Jessica. They loved doing crafts. We were able to take our trailer up to the their house so they would come over and do games and crafts. They loved to spend the night with us in the trailer. It was a special time.

Along came Symone, and then Brittney, making six granddaughters. Forest was our first grandson. Then Brian, then came Kody, Korey, Olivia and Knox. What a blessing. In 1991 I didn't think I would get to see my last three children graduate, let alone see my great grandchildren.

Kurt and Sheryl moved to Alaska, so we had to go see Kody before he grew up. We flew up to Alaska, and Kurt and family met us at the airport with shorts on. It was still sunny at midnight. I had a coat and was freezing. We had a great time. Went and spent some time in a cottage and did some tourist things. It was hard to say goodbye as I wasn't sure when I would see them again. They ended up coming back to California, so we did get to spend time with them.

Joanne lived in Portland, so we didn't spend as much time with Symone as I would have liked to when she was a baby, but when she got older we did a lot of fun things together. One great memory was when I had Symone and Brian come spend the night in our trailer. We were parked up at Michael's mom's and we had to put a new floor in the trailer. We ended up tearing the whole floor up so we just had studs, and the kids would jump from one place to another. We laughed at them as they made it look so funny. It is a great memory.

We lived in the fifth wheel for five years, working at Bible camps and churches helping out as we could. We would work and they gave us a place to park. Then we were able to work as missionaries along the Mexican border. They had radio stations from Brownsville TX to Yuma AZ. When we got to Pharr TX, we lived behind the radio station in our fifth wheel for awhile. Then we bought a 35 x 12 ft Park Model. We lived there for 9 years. It was a cute little house and it worked well. We also had a 24 foot fifth wheel to go to the radio stations all along the Mexican border, fixing them when they broke down. The Lord blessed us with two new radio stations here in Oregon so we got to spend time with them as we were building the stations.

Pharr TX is the only place I lived that the windows were wet on the outside and it was not even raining. The humidity was so high that you got wet just going outside. The other thing that bothered me was at Christmas it was quite often in the 80's and it just didn't feel like Christmas. Then one year on Christmas Eve it snowed and stuck to the ground until noon on Christmas day. That was a fun Christmas.

Being that most Christmases were in the 80's, I decided to take some friends to Podray Island to have brunch on Christmas day. The plan was to take pictures of us on the beach on Christmas. We got up that morning and it was cold out and rainy so that didn't work out too well. We went on the beach for about five minutes, then headed to the warm car.

In our travels we had quite a lot of experiences. We have spent the night on the side of the road many times. One time we lost a wheel on the express way and broke our axle. The tire almost hit another car, but missed. It had rolled across our side, then over to oncoming traffic. Michael always said there was an angel watching over us. He had looked back on the road, and there was not a car in sight, then a truck with a dog pulled up along side of us and pointed to the tire. Michael look down and saw the tire was at an angle, and when he look up the truck was gone. We were then towed to a tire place in a little tiny town, and had to spend three nights there. We had a small generator that we could use for TV if we wanted to, but we had to use the big one for air conditioning, and we didn't know what to do if we ran out of gas. It would get hot because it was in the hundred's. It was quite miserable. We finally got the trailer fixed and back on the road. Another thing we didn't realize is that our truck had a hard time pulling the RV up hills, so when we hit the mountains we would just creep up them, then when we came down it wanted to push us. We had a few breakdowns because of that. One morning we woke up and looked out the window, and we were surrounded by Buffalo. It was neat, but it did hold up our leaving.

Chips our dog traveled with us. He was quite the traveler. If the truck started up, he was there, and if you left the door open, he would jump right in. Sometimes he got in other people's trucks too. When we traveled, I would take carrots for a snack, and he loved them. I would give Michael one, and then Chips one, he would chew his down, then wait for us to finish ours. Then he'd look for another one.

We lived in the fifth wheel for five years working at Bible camps and churches helping out as we could. We would work, and they gave us a place to park. Then we were able to work as missionaries along the Mexican border. We were there only a short time when Kitty and Jimmy came, they lived in the backyard with us.

The Sowers on Wheels came to the station to do work for us. That is the same group we belonged to. Once they ran out of things to do for the station, so they built us a deck to go across the front of out trailer. Then Jimmy and Kitty were given a hot tub, so we put it over there on the deck. It was great, and I think Kitty and I used it more than anyone else. Her granddaughter came and spent some time with us, so she would swim in it. Then the next time she came she was too big, so she just sit in it like us old folks.

I decided to put a garden in behind our trailer. The vegetables didn't do well, as it was so hot, but the flowers did well. Michael built me a pergola for me to climb Jasmine on. I loved it. Then he put a watering system in. It really was quite nice. I put trees all around it because the wind blew so hard there. So that helped block it.

One night Michael had to go fix a radio station, and I was by myself with our dog Chips. We had some vandalism at the front of the station before, so when I saw a car pull in, then turn his lights off, then back on, I was suspicious. Then he did it again, so I decided to go check out the station to make sure they weren't doing something to the front of the station. I took the dog, and the gun we had, and walked all around the station. It was good. When Michael got home I told him what I did. He was worried that I had done such a stupid thing. Then he told me the gun didn't have any bullets in it as he had shot a skunk and never reloaded it. Well I didn't do that again. A short time later they put a fence around five acres of the forty, and put up an electric gate so no one could come in unless invited. That did make me feel safer. We had a sugar cane field next to us, and Mexico was only a mile away, so illegals would hide in the field.

Living behind the station, we were able to use the kitchen and dinning room. We would have friends over to play games and eat. It was a lot of fun. We also put up a Christmas tree in the dinning area. One day a large box showed up under the tree, I never thought about it being mine, then on Christmas day Michael had me open it. It was from our children, it was a rocker for our house. I love it and still have it in our front room in this house.

A few major things happened while living there, my heart decided to get weaker, so they decided to put in a pace maker and defibrillator. I could hardly do anything before, but after they put that in I was like the energizer bunny. Michael called me his bionic babe. Then my mother went home to be with the Lord. That was a hard time, but I know she was ready to go. She had Parkinson's disease for a long time, and she hurt all the time. I didn't want that for her, but we do miss her. Our Chips passed away, and we do miss him too. He was a wonderful dog and very faithful to us. We have had two dogs Angel and now Trooper. We love them, but Chips was special.

We needed to raise more support because we were living off of Michael's retirement from the Air Force. It came to a point that it was not enough. We were headed to Yuma Arizona and were praying about it. On our way back, Michael got a call from a friend that we were going to stop to visit, and he asked if he would consider putting in for a paying job in Dallas Texas. He did, and he got the job. So two weeks later, we moved to Dallas. We lived there for 10 years. We bought a house, but we had no furniture so, I went to yard sales. It wasn't long before we had a houseful. Michael called it yard sale decorations, and it was fun. When we left, I had three yard sales, and made $2000 to help get us set up here in Oregon.

A year later Jana and her family moved there. She is my sister's daughter, so when Phyllis came to visit them, Paul and her would stay with us. They came at Christmas and spring just after school got out. It was a wonderful sister time, and I think it grew us closer than we have ever been. We did games and puzzles, which I enjoy a lot.

I joined a quilt group there. I had messed around with it, but never really got serious until then. Since I started Quilting, I have made many quilts. So far I made one for Jessica, Kristin, Kourtney, Britney, and Olivia. I have done several wall hangings and a few quilts for us. The other thing that was neat was I got to go sing with a couple of lady's at a nursing home. It really was a blessing to hear them sing with us they loved the old Hymns. We did crafts, and at Easter we decorated hats and had an Easter parade. It was a lot of fun.

I made many friends there, and we had a wonderful church, but Oregon was calling me to come back. Texas was fine, but I missed the trees, the mountains, and most of all my kids. So I talked Michael into retiring early so we could go home. It is the best thing we have done, I enjoy the time I have with my children. We are able to go camping a lot in the summer and spend time with our friends. Michael keeps busy with his ham radio, and all the clubs he belongs to, including train clubs. I go to a Bible study once a week, and we do one together with a group from our church. We have made more friends through the studies.

Which reminds me, an amazing thing that happened when we were in Texas. I met this neat lady at a quilt group, and found out she was from Salem Oregon. They had been in Texas for about two years. I told her I wanted to go back, and she did too because her family all live here. Well she made it before I did. We met up, and Cheryl and Bob became great friends. We ended up buying a house about fifteen minutes away, and it was great. Then Bob passed away and Cheryl decided to sell her house and get a smaller one. She ended up moving close to her sister, and about one hour away from me. I thought I wouldn't see her much, but so far we have been able to spend as much time as we did when she was close.

I have had a bucket list, and Branson was on it. We got to go about six years ago for our anniversary. My next thing on the list was a cruise, and we did that in 2015. I still had my Hawaii trip, and Michael felt that would never happen, but I kept bugging him. One day my friends

Sue and Cheryl said they would love to go so, why can't we just go. So I told Michael we were going to look into it. That night he came home and told me he had already set it up to go in October, and he was going to surprise me on my Birthday. Well I messed that up, and he felt bad because the girls didn't want to go because they had already been there. Sue's husband didn't want to go, and Cheryl didn't want to go by herself. Anyway Michael set up a trip for just us girls to cruise to Mexico in February. He is a wonderful husband.

A couple of years ago, I told my children that when I turned eighty I wanted to do the chicken dance. I will be seventy-nine in December, so I only have one year before my eightieth birthday. Not sure where the time has gone. Life is short and unpredictable. I had to go through some rough times, but I believe they have made me stronger and closer to God. When life is easy, I think, "I can do it myself." Then the Lord reminds me that He is in control. Man gave me six months to live, and God gave me thirty years. I have been able to see all my six children grow up and become adults. I am so proud of them. Also, I am proud of my twelve grandchildren, and five great grandchildren. One is already in Heaven waiting for me. It will be a blessed time when I see Genesis, our little angel.

In 1949 I asked Jesus into my heart to be my Lord and Savior. I need to share with you how you can do the same. It is very easy. You know, we are all sinners, but when you ask Him to be your Savior, we are sinners saved by Grace. I could never be perfect, but He took my sins and died on the cross just for me. That is so awesome!

It is an easy 3 steps:

1. God loves you and has a plan for you. *"Jesus said, I came that they may have life and have it abundantly." (John 10:10)* So we need to accept who God is.

2. We have all done and thought bad things, which the Bible calls sin. *"All have sinned and fallen short of the glory of God."* (Romans 3:23) So we must believe.

3. God sent His Son to die for my sins. *"Christ died for our sins. He was buried. He was raised on the third day, according*

to the Scriptures." (1 Corinthians 15:3-4)

Jesus is the only way to God, Jesus said, *"I am the way and the truth, and the life; no one comes to the Father, but through Me."* (John 14:6)

We can't earn salvation; we are saved by God's grace when we have faith in His Son.